1. Cheese grits.

2. We're the reason God created football.

3. World's last outpost of good manners.

4. Humidity eliminates need for expensive home sauna.

5. You can put a license tag on anything, drive it down the road, and no one will stop you.

6. Sweet tea.

—⦙—

7. Barbecue.

8. Unlike less-fun Yankee states, it only takes one snowflake to create a state-wide holiday.

9. Supermarkets have cute names like Piggly Wiggly and Winn-Dixie.

10. No official limit on height of hair-do's.

—⁂—

11. Children actually address adults using the epithets sir and ma'am.

12. Police officers greet you by name when pulling you over for a traffic violation.

13. Cultural trends take hold at a leisurely pace so everyone can get on board.

14. Crocuses come up before the last Christmas decorations are down.

15. New York and California not taken seriously.

16. Gulf beaches.

—⁓—

17. Everyone knows how to tell a good story.

18. Politics are more entertaining than in other states.

—⁂—

19. The Auburn–Alabama game.

20. Front porches.

—◈—

21. Back porches.

—◈—

22. Corn on the cob.

23. We have our own way of tawkin'.

—∿—

24. We have our own music.

25. More family reunions than any other state.

26. Best darn joke tellers in the world.

27. Plenty of elbow room.

—~~—

28. Fried pie.

29. People still know how to dress up.

30. At every get-together, there's always someone who can pick a guitar.

31. Unlike hum-drum Yankee supper tables, there's no skimping on side dishes.

32. Vintage automobiles are given the respect they deserve.

33. Highest per capita cosmetic skills in the nation.

34. More books and songs written about Alabama than any other state.

35. Azaleas.

—◦◦◦—

36. Fried okra.

—◦◦◦—

37. Corn bread.

38. Farmer's markets.

—◆—

39. Flea markets.

40. Neighbors rarely come over empty-handed.

41. If you break down on the side of the road, someone will always stop to help.

42. Soda pop brands have more colorful names, like Nehi and Grapico.

43. No part of a pig ever goes to waste.

—⁂—

44. Church suppers on the ground.

45. Citizens generally know the difference between right and wrong.

46. Wild blackberries.

—⁓—

47. Bluebirds in spring.

48. Children actually use the quaint expressions please and thank you.

49. Tent revivals.

—◆—

50. River rats.

51. People don't generally pass through, they come to stay.

52. Small-talk skill level highest in nation.

53. Handshakes still effective in business dealings.

54. We might fight but we always make up.

55. Fishing that borders on religious experience.

56. Knowing someone will always hold the door for you.

57. 365-day golfing season.

58. Palm trees, dogwoods, sycamores, live oaks, fig trees, sweet gums, and magnolias.

59. Never a shortage of advice on any subject.

—∿—

60. Traffic laws subject to individual interpretation.

61. Central air.

---~~~---

62. Sweet potato pie.

63. Misty mornings in the mountains.

—⁂—

64. Wild muscadines.

65. Dirt-track racing.

—◊◊◊—

66. Family recipes.

67. Sunsets in November.

—◆◆◆—

68. Red-tailed hawks.

69. Homemade ice cream.

—〰—

70. Peach cobbler.

71. Snow flurries on Thanksgiving.

—ᴧᴧᴧ—

72. Heat waves on Thanksgiving.

73. No legal limit on quantity of exterior Christmas lights per household.

74. There are still people who talk without cussing.

—◆◆◆—

75. For those who must cuss, wide array of original expletives available.

76. Backyard gardens.

—◊—

77. Sawmill gravy.

78. Neighborhood block parties.

—∾—

79. Volunteer fire departments.

80. Mayors who conveniently also sell insurance and used cars.

—∾—

81. Camellias blooming in February.

82. 'Nanner puddin'.

—⧋—

83. Mee-maw's coconut cake.

84. Pa-paw's tomatoes.

—∾—

85. Folks know your mamma and daddy and their mammas and daddies.

86. Bluegrass festivals.

—⚬⚬⚬—

87. Going barefoot in March.

88. Butter beans.

—⁓—

89. Fried catfish.

—⁓—

90. Certain homemade beverages.

91. Choice cockroach specimens guaranteed to scare the wits out of unsuspecting Yankees.

92. High ratio of morning radio shows with host named Bubba.

—〰—

93. Siestas on summer afternoons.

94. Strangers say hello on the street and, instead of running in the opposite direction, you say hello back.

95. Home to one of the seven wonders of the world: the infield at Talladega on race day.

96. Misguided national news coverage of state keeps obnoxiously heavy, environmentally damaging tourist traffic to a minimum.

97. Children grow up bilingual, speaking both English and Southern.

98. State leads the way in culinary presentation of the peanut.

99. Women named Velma.

100. Men named J.B., J.R., J.D., J.P., J.C., J.T., or J.W.

101. You can leave Alabama, but you'll always come back home.